THE BLOOD CHOIR

THE BLOOD CHOIR

Tim Liardet

seren

Seren is the book imprint of
Poetry Wales Press Ltd
57 Nolton Street, Bridgend, Wales, CF31 3AE
www.seren-books.com

ISBN 1-85411-414-X

A CIP record for this title is available from the British Library.

The publisher acknowledges the financial assistance
of the Welsh Books Council.

Printed in Hoefler Text by Bell & Bain Ltd, Glasgow.

Cover: La Romería de San Isidro (detail) by Goya
© Prado Museum, Madrid

CONTENTS

For the Seven Hundred and Forty Ninth Species
    of Barbed Wire   9
Spaniels in a Field of Kale   10
The Blood Choir   11
The Unveiling   16
Loy's Return   17
The Ailing   18
The Language School   19
Going into the Yellow   21
The Vaults   22
The Echoists   23
Wasps   24
The Expulsion of X   25
A Shithouse Reverie   26
Opera of Yawns   27
Spider-ballet   29
Martianism   30
Shoe Gazing   31
Art   32
The Lumbar Region   33
Archia, Archia   34
Foot and Mouth   35
The Contagion   36
Why Dunwoody Smashed Every Pane of the
    Stained Glass Window   39
Distilling   40
Playing Hangman   41
Lines for the Bird that Flew into the Prison   43
The Missionary Position   44
Psychosis   46
The Physics of Chinese-wrestling   47
The Uses of Pepper   48
Music   49
Ganja   50

Hyperactive   51
Anatomy of the Flat   52
Water-walking   54
The Fluttering-place   55
At Dusk, You Can Hear the Men Calling   60
Ground Bass   61

Acknowledgements   69

Barbed wire can be considered a decisive stage in the history of virtualising the political management of space. Yet, the symbol of power, which represents the capacity to enclose space, tends to weaken; it becomes a negative symbol of a brutal sovereignty...

– Olivier Razac, *Barbed Wire: A Political History*

The deeper 'layers' of the psyche lose their individual uniqueness as they retreat farther and farther into the darkness. 'Lower down', that is to say, as they approach the autonomous functional system, they become increasingly collective until they are universalised and extinguished in the body's materiality, that is, in chemical substances. The body's carbon is simply carbon. Hence 'at bottom' the psyche is simply world...

– C.G. Jung, *The Archetypes and the Collective Unconscious*

Painting (like poetry) selects from among the universal that which it judges most appropriate for its purpose. It unites in a single imaginary being circumstances and characters which nature presents distributed in many, and it is in this unity that true imitation is achieved, by which the artist acquires the title of inventor and not that of servile copyist.

– Francisco Goya, *Diario de Madrid, 1799*

FOR THE SEVEN HUNDRED AND FORTY NINTH SPECIES OF BARBED WIRE

Only the rain can cling to it, snatched away
by a rumour of air thickening then passing.
Let a hand try the same, we're told, and a trap

of razors will spring and close, spring and close.
(In it, they say, the body of a jackdaw left its feet
thirty metres from its head, which nonetheless

turned to address them: "... only half of us can make it
over the wire, half in the world, half out,
though the pale gas of morning rises on either side.")

Think of it: a contraption of blades coiled
along the top of the towering fence erected between
six hundred young men and their birthright.

One side of it thrive all the indices
of hunger, the other the many sorts of worldly apple.

SPANIELS IN A FIELD OF KALE

The two spaniels leaping and flying
like shadow and leaper, like leaper and shadow
sent in wider and wider circles,
the more they leap about, and chase
each other through the mile-wide depths of choppy kale,
the more they might be mistaken for
an upblown leaf, a lifted edge that balances
its catchment of light briefly like their coats
parting to the skin in the wind's combs
which cross the heath like a search-party, extending
the eerie coastline of the prison fence.
The logic of them, flopping and collapsing, flies
out in a northerly direction towards the last outcrops
of Scapa Flow, or keeps going with the rafts
of overushing altocumulus due west
to the land floes of Inishbofin, east to Orford Ness
or south to the lip of the Lizard, where it hovers panting
over the odd ellipsis of Land's End;
this before it takes the whole flight on rewind,
tracing it phase by phase until the dogs
refind the channel they have trodden flat
in the blowing field where the kale
springs up again in front of them, untrampled.
The logic of their leaping takes
the flight again, and then again, as if each flight
is the exercise without which its belly
would drag too close to the ground,
and those tresses in earthbound flight become
a slip-leash, a sort of flowing yoke built around
the features of a little prune face
and mouthful of yappy snarls.

THE BLOOD CHOIR

After Goya

I

Consider how a young man sheds his name
and number, his boot blister and tattoo,

his lisp, his wrist-scar and dental history;
how he sheds, in short, all that could not

be anyone's but his, the ancient encryption
of his fingerprint, the mole on the ball of his foot.

It is a terrible thing to witness the speed with which
he and twenty other inmates are drawn up,

stumbling backwards, into one another; how they grow
eerily identical webbed feet, webbed fingers,

webbed ears, and melt their bone-marrow down
to the kind of red glue that welds them together

at the pelvis, the abdomen and the chest
as if, well, some slow-moving animal penned

by a single rope, tugging at each wrist; some rhythm
of oars rowed, without a drum; some engine

which drives a sort of spirit replica straight through
the savage razors of the wire without a scratch.

II

The one, usually the strongest, the one
with the large X smeared on his forehead

invisibly in red, there for good however much
he tries to wash it off, the one who stands

above the rest at six foot three, the broadest,
most bullish-loud, who changes shape,

and always wears, like all the rest,
the identical bottle-green shirt, green trousers,

standard issue boots, mandatory snarl,
who changes shape in mind and in physique,

estranged self, say, into sea-inhabiting being,
willing ear into something with eight, no, fourteen arms,

something that leans its body weight forward
with no control of either limb or energy

but scrambles a disk of prison numbers,
carrying under each of its fourteen arms the head

of another grinning boy who carries
under each of his fourteen arms another grinning head.

III

The flash-point at the centre is red, red
as the sleep of reason. Note how

quickly the fluid in the ball-joints welds
hip-girdle to hip-girdle, their finger-bones thread

each other's rings, arms each other's sleeves;
how they seem to stand at roughly the same height

and swing their knuckles to roughly the same depth
as if hinged upon the same fine shank:

note how, when it shouts, there are twenty mouths
drawing on one capacity to breathe;

how its outer stockade is comprised
of every slightest elbow-movement that was made

in the last thirty seconds, seen all at once,
as if its dead weight were evolving the lightness

of a gossamer wing-beat, lifting it off the ground.
A warm wind blows all around it, blowing

hair in towards the centre. It bellows, dies,
looks down, drums the rubber of its many feet.

IV

How can it be said to have any shape at all,
lacking love, asks the prison chaplain? Look how

it assembles, in its war-paint of tattoos:
long-necked and flatfooted, distorted as though

by a fairground mirror, growing hard pads
exactly where it needs them, developing

all that upper muscle, plates beneath the skin
and helmets so ridged they seem more like

mouldings of bone beneath the shaven scalp;
and pale, well yes, pale from a diet of dross

and having grown so long and awkwardly
in the dark, but strong, for having spurned love

as so much squandered oxygen, a Grimm's
fairy tale for the snug, a myth

not sticking to it – see how it stands, equipped
with the perfect armour of scorn, plus

steel elbows and steel knuckles, perfect
for the world it must enter and smash to bits.

V

Like something dying back, withdrawing once it has
gone out perhaps as far as it can go,

now dying back. Having flourished red,
having pitched into wilderness, the more its shouts

were wrung to liquid, the more it colonized space;
now dying back. See how the body of it

yields at the centre, and disassembles; how it first
drummed up its dream of sovereignty and now

gives it up, quietly; how it breaks apart, leaving
one boy to smile among his freckles

like the patron saint of shrinking violets,
another to rub his neck, one to blow his nose

and one to sigh, others to turn away, as if surprised
by daylight after the matinée, flung clear...

This is how the organism (having pulled and tossed
in its chains) detaches its many body parts

and disperses them towards some sort of roll-call:
Allam, Dunwoody, Cuedjoe, Burke,

THE UNVEILING

But Quraishi's appalling breast exposes
the wonders of the naturally excessive
(...with a theatrical lift of his shirt)
to the leaning forward and leaning back of those

who've seen it before but want to see it again,
who first look into it, then sway away, as if
laughter distils into one response
revulsion and awe, recoil and the drawn-

by-sensors-to-a-fellow-spirit, taboo and touch,
the forbidden, soft vernacular of touch:
it is the pretext by which Quraishi's
two hundred and fifty overweening pounds achieve

a bordello status, more bruise than areola,
the spider-woman's kimono-secret:
whatever it is, whatever it is not,
he tenders it deliberately with a sort

of queasy benediction. The old gaol is suddenly
like a canvas over them about to flap away.
And Quraishi is pestered, pestered
for this vast and inverted flaccidness as if it offered
milk for the shoving litter, milk for the starved.

LOY'S RETURN

To be on your back, says Loy, mashed, while the stuccoed
saloon bar lurches up and dreams it floats
or dips into the wave, and the room goes bending and rolling;

to be nose-up in one boot, while the barmaid calls to you
for some unknown reason in French, *fucking* French.
Nu, this; *Vu* that. *Bonwee* or *Bonwat*, or something

like that. To claw your way up from the floor of the gents
by the taps, says Loy, setting off the hand-drier
to which you mouth a greeting, then drop back,

and having learned how tricky swimming is
after seven years and three months, a week,
a day, three hours inside, he says, to wake to find yourself

staring up from under water and holding your breath
until there's not a bubble to tell anyone you're there,
not a *fucking* bubble, if you'll pardon the French.

THE AILING

Strange how the dropped crockery does not break
nor reach the floor, and no one notices. Here in this place
of locked cells and of lines kept reassuringly straight

things grow comfortable very slowly. The thought
swims in water brought to the boil, the huge and nameless event
steps in through the wall, and no one notices.

The click of the guard's shoe cannot quite catch up with
its metal tip. What might be a film plays in silence....
And rueful Wilbur's sentence? Oh, a thousand years, served

in hair-fall and scissor-snips, if snip could catch the scissors
and he could remember how to play. Look how his arms
are secured behind his back, and hands slightly more

eager than his own have been fed through his sleeves
to yawn the bow softly across his cello.
Somewhere, years back, the first note snivels.

THE LANGUAGE SCHOOL

I

The charges might as well be read out
in Chinese, Bantu or Dravidian

or not be read at all – they drift, they loop
like light that cannot turn a corner

or soundwaves that bend in and out
of some fidelity to the original. To whom

do they cling? Another dumbstruck boy
who does not speak the English they speak

or even hear it – all nape and haircut, sat
folded up in a Jesuit clasp

with hands in his armpits, perusing
with a sort of thick-lipped composure

the platypus-nose of his left trainer, as if it had
evolved out of kilter with the rest.

II

No is the blank, the zero, the lumpy zilch,
the bijou fuck-all the question solicits

and wishes-for: the litany, the plural of no.
It is the answer the question anticipates

before asking itself, surrounding no.
Do you have anything to say in your own defence?

The hiatus, the answer-in-minus scans
the many milliseconds of a second

that hang like a threat, scaring it
way up into the corner of articulation

where it ceases to exist.
Without fuss, or noise, or anything,

without changing expression or looking up
the only yes there is nods to a no.

GOING INTO THE YELLOW

When it came to Conrad's map it wasn't the expanses of red
or the areas of green or of orange or purple,
I was going into the yellow. Dead centre.
The commission was clear: to confront a population
of sentenced and resentful men (invisibly roped)
who, as they entered, seemed too lumbering huge
for the space they occupied, and to engage them, and teach
the gentle arts of self-expression, hand to heart,
biro-end to teeth... I felt like a man sent to fix, say,
a ten-by-three mile rupture in the side of the Zambezi dam
with a tube of calk, dental floss, a hammer and nails
and an endless chain of paper bags that filled up and burst;
the thrown-into-the-gap, the heaped, the washed away,
as quickly dissolving sandbags of woeful words.

THE VAULTS

Down, down, deeper and deeper down, entering
the prison's underground chamber where fear is a sort
of aloe sapping the tongue, on the brink of zero hour:
every heavy iron gate which has to be unlocked and locked
wails on its hinges, wails for its want of lubrication,
then clank-echoes shut, then clank-echoes shut,
the last of eight heavy gates behind us clank-echoes shut.
Claustrophobia, no falsifying dream – it is as if
we are welded into the hold, the lid in its seals,
and the chamber itself is about to flood,
to flood: armed with counted pencils, protractors and Donne,
we are sombre when we move up in masks to our places as
a highpitched intensifying note (become
intolerable) passes out of human hearing.

THE ECHOISTS

They began by repeating all my words.
Now don't do that, please; *now don't do that, pleeeese...*
Whatever I tried to teach them, it was sent back
on its privileged plate untouched.

Before long, each statement and its echo became
one utterance. Whatever I said set off
their high-pitched and ironic echolalia
struck in the key of an old man's falsetto croaks

as if to say that anything I might choose to say
was in dire need of counterpoise. I, I; *I, I...*
I mean to say, I mean...; *I mean to say, I meeeene...*
The echo got glued to every word, got stuck

like the man who went on hiccoughing for twenty years
and still hasn't quit. Long after I left them
behind razor wire, tall gates and bars the echoists
like tones in the wilderness, like semitones,

continue supplying on one frequency the echo
to the word. The echo clings to my explodents
and my glottal-stops, as it will for ten,
for twenty years, for the rest of my life.

The echo continues to spasm among
the dipped-in-light roots of my vocal chords,
a sort of eerie and distorting in-built heckle
forever speaking at the edges of its own sound

and weighing every word for its ingredient truth
as if to remind us language only ever belongs
to its blind creators, and the lake we drink at is full
of water and undrinkable water.

WASPS

Because wasps disregard the razors of the prison fence
when they drift indoors, drawn
by the confusion of odours
boredom remorselessly mixes into one – the allure
of a sticky linctus-bottle, say,
or of bacteria fermenting, patient to form a skin –
spuds turning ever so slowly into soldier-crabs – this is a happening,
an *event*, between the great lapses of concentration.
There is panic, and voices raised, a swarming across the room;
the latest wasp chased down the glass
by nine, ten, no, fifteen men
for whom the fence is obstacle
and (to junkets of cheering) swatted, and swatted, and swatted,
until something is finally satisfied,
beaten to silence, or otherwise put to sleep.

Out of earshot, a voice says: "...because you are the miracle
of engineering sprung beneath your fuselage
of tiger hoops, so sleek, so exquisitely evolved...
we must hate you; because you fizz between
the panes and thump about and dream our spaces your kingdom
we must leave you wrecked
in your entrails – because brindled gold was your birthright
and purpose, a purpose indifferent to us;
because you were too brazen, too beautiful, too *perfect*."

THE EXPULSION OF X

Gated, expelled, caught wandering in his shirt
or out of it, we conjecture, he and his ballast of books,
his style of teaching and shoulder-length hair
– what squealed its clue on the board, and left it there –
are locked forever outside the prison gates.
And we, his colleagues, told we do not need
to know why. And cannot ask. He is kept out
from a place built more for ensuring the culpable
are kept in, and eighty iron gates that separate
each corridor from the next shut one by one
against our curiosity to a deafening *shshshsh*...
We learn the art of not knowing. How what lies
in the sterile zone at the core of army language
compresses a region of sky within its cage-sides,
crossed by a flash-flood of altocumuli;
how it gets rid for good of the indolent sinner
and sends him out cupping his privates.
The airbrushes start with his feet, his knees.
They reach his waist, his chest. They reach his head
and we pick through his effects for clues:
his doctoral thesis had been entitled *The horror film*
and how it disguises its narrative purpose.
And he liked to hold the frames, he said, hovering there
on pause: look into them, discern a further detail
never quite noticed before, he said, drawn
to the subtler species of horror that
seems to play with something you already know
or half know, in your toes. Like the frame
in which, along with the doomed hero, what you assume's
an albino child about to turn around and smile
from the very back of her deep hood is
a dwarf eighty years old, who does not necessarily
mean you well. That turning around
again and again. That face. On slow-mo.

A SHITHOUSE REVERIE

I have often been afraid, but these early morning yells
exchanged like ritual blows set every single hair of me
on end, a spider of hair treading my nape, fear

staring from every hair – flung, into the early air,
from cell-window to cell-window like blades winnowing
and sharpening each other half way across (...while I

prepared myself in the toilet best as I could) the yells
called to the stifled yell in me suggesting I get
my whole body out double quick; they pushed back the bones

in my face through realignment after realignment
to where, at four years old, I stumbled into the fetch
of the wave that sucked me down beyond my father's reach

and held me under with open eyes, while my hair swarmed
all around me like an electric shock, and I looked
into the mirror of water that would not look back.

OPERA OF YAWNS

I

When their largely unused bodies slump
at desks, one yawn sets off the next which sets off

the next which sets off the next until there is only
this miming-time of mouths. And they fall, they fall,

the thirteen of them, into a lazy sort
of composition which, from where I stand, most resembles

a pastiche of the Last Supper, a company of prisoners
leaning and sprawling into its place – mild Bartholomew,

James the Younger and Andrew, feeling their prickly scalps;
Judas leaning on one elbow, suffering his barber-embargo;

Peter yawning his way through his crop of accusations
while the circuit of the yawn has reached quiet Matthew,

sad Thaddeus, Simon and the others, our Christ-like Quraishi
haloed by the light-bulb. From here, for now,

they appear of supernatural size, serving their time
by shifting this way and that, shifting this way and that

and yawning for the absence of news, a little way off,
as yet, from the garden of the hacked ear.

II

Or else it might be a mime of men laughing
at some missed, too-long-to-follow and encoded

joke, a miming of the voice-loss aria...
and all they have from which to read the words

is the hooded autocue which drops into their minds
white slide after white slide, a jerked

shuttering of wiped whiteness through which they stare
to the white wall, to ever more widening particles

of white, without feature or plot, on which only
great operas of crime can possibly be projected

with huge exaggeration... the eye open, the retina asleep.
And they yawn, and they yawn, and they dredge

the silt for the deepest yawn of all
as if, for every depth they reach, they mouth the highest note

and hold this posture in which they might conserve
a certain sort of power from knowing there is

air, three inch-thick glass and a safety curtain
between them and the auditorium of the deaf.

SPIDER-BALLET

Lobotomised by boredom since
they discovered there was nothing much to listen to
they lift up their heavy desks on their knees
and crash them down, lift up one by a leg
high into the air – a drama – look out
of the window and stretch, and yawn, or pace, and start
to shove each other hard and wrestle down a head
beneath an arm, and yawn again, and shout
and slowly, slowly, as though the dust of prison ennui
can fertilise the growth of extra legs,
start to climb the wall, exploiting the grip
of those thick rubber soles as if to make
weird shadows in the upturned light,
stepping across the ceiling with long spidery strides.

MARTIANISM

The exercise, they must grasp, is to see like a visitor
on his first visit to the planet, bewildered
by the windy squeal of the telephone;
windows that flash and ride upon a man's nose, like heliographs;
time's vacuum throbbing on the wrist.

I must explain this to a room of men whose cropped heads
expose the now-healed but savage route-map
of the street-war, the blasted frond of their septums;
pupils that go in and out like expeditions, bold but poorly financed,
to the edge of the world where they pause.

Listen. Their raised voices frighten this cold room
out of its accoustics, with the sort of slurred tongueless storm
of language indigenous to these parts,
from which no meaning can be picked out.
So we meet it for the first time, the uneasy handclasp between us,

in need of interpreters, gifts. "Your boots,
when you walk," they say, "squeak so loud, it sounds
like they're filled with water, like there's water in every squeak."
As if I bring little bootfuls, oozing at my eyelets,
they stare at me like I've walked off some mile-wide cosmic lake.

"You squelch on," they imply, "we'll cling together on dry land."
There is a planet here, for sure, and a meeting
and reception, teacher and prisoner stuffed full
of overture and caution, pink flags, uncertain who visits, who
is visited. We look at each other amazed.

SHOE GAZING

McStein has a facial scar and mannerly sense,
Sol, so loud, in a perpetual lather;
Hodgkins's sly, intelligent, furtive way
the counterpoint to Bradley's manic brain;
Aziz, his inoffensive glissando of laugh;
Randals, infallibly drawn to the weak –

One by one, I dream them, whose crimes
rattle and bump behind them like a cortège of tin cans.
Their faces – I don't know how to say this –
are turning into mine. That smile.
It started and now it cannot stop.
A potential is mirrored like a shadow. It falls, like rain,

in the spaces between assumptions
and threads the body's interstices, goes into your bones.
Look. They have found my new shoes
and squabble, trying to read the label.
Into their white-as-sea-foam trainers,
earned for good behaviour, I slip an overcautious foot.

ART

Most memorable they ever had, says Feysal, brought
to every cell along with the hookah smoke
a sense of the all-providing – the patchwork of Rizzlas swaddling

enough rich Virginia and Moroccan Red to becalm
the six hundred, lowered on the shreds of a prison towel
from cell window to cell window under cover

of the darkness in which it glowed and burned down
to a loaded ochra of ash, says Feysal, drained
of the well-being that at length reaches the nerve ends,

at length reaches the hair-roots, reaches the toes.
All were amiable, he says, they learned to think
in tiers, and for weeks tried to get the savouring of it out

of their heads onto the wall, scratched on the cell-door,
on folders, wherever there was space, and it was like
each image was a sort of blind attempt to pin the horns

in the right place, full of something he couldn't quite
put a finger on, sort of weird and childish, full of whatever it is
cave paintings are full of, orange and blood-red.

THE LUMBAR REGION

Something cracked in the lumbar region
beneath the osteopath's unwitting touch
and three other selves slithered out of him
with the same thick head of hair
and the same eye-colour and same weight
but very different expressions.

One was unable to look to his left
and one unable to look to his right
and one leaned sideways hugging his feet
and all of them tried to steal a breath
and, for a moment, they were one man
and then they all stepped out of one another.

But he was the one at whose ear
the other three kept on and on
pestering and whingeing and accusing
as if he was the wickedest and eldest
who needed reminding hourly
of what he had done, of what he had done.

Beyond them, whole blocks of men
had to be kept from him for his own good
as if he had wiped away their crimes;
in the confinement of the top floor
he was locked behind glass and steel, through which
often all three spoke to him at once:

her hair, her tears, one said, oh her laid out
among her metres of curls, she seemed so young;
I watched, one said, I watched, I watched;
I knew you knew I knew, said one, you knew I knew.
Whatever you did to our mother, they say,
now there is nothing of us from the waist down.

ARCHIA, ARCHIA

The Archia frisked when she comes to visit
the prison, explains Renu, is not the Archia
released back into the world by the prison timer switch:

that teeshirt and those faded jeans, breasts a-tilt,
those coils of heavy hair half let down, half held up
by pins, says Renu, that lipgloss and attitude perched some way

along the length of a squint-making cigarette
(...lifting every bowed head in the Visitors' Room)
are shed, half way back, when she changes in her old Peugeot

and wraps herself to the chin in her hijab and the cloth-folds
which actually reduce her size, in proportion to the opening
she could any minute pass through, close or let

cast more fully over her, the second timer-switch going off:
sombre, covered to the ankles, cauled in the drapery
of an ancient patronage, says Renu, it's like she is

released by one time switch, admitted by another:
so she must smuggle herself out, smuggle herself in
or stay exactly where she is, rocked by two-way juggernauts.

FOOT AND MOUTH

One ran, one trotted, one fell silent, one was mute,
two – by trotting or running – *spoke*;
they leapt the truck's tail-gate and the wire.
One placed a language in the other's feet
like tendons, like muscles, like spring...

beast and boy escaping from the herd.
The trucks of soon-to-be-slaughtered cows
were carriers of all our harms, so many snorting
at the blow-hole it seemed a whole country
was hauled behind them, tearing up roots.

The trucks passed the prison early, in convoy,
when men were busy seeking for a shoe,
an overcoat slumped in the lights like a body,
six hundred subtracting an empty bed.
That shred of standard issue shirt snagged on wire

thought to be impassable – *he must have vaulted
it*, they said, *the fucker must have flown* –
seemed something alert was trying to say
that where there's a multitude there is also one
who'll leave its bright rags to flap:

these were the rags from which the boy
had ripped himself clear and was already a mile
over the heath, at the very moment a calf
almost absurdly leggy and vulnerable
tip-tapped across a hooting motorway.

THE CONTAGION

I

As if dumped into the cholera pits, the latest load
of slaughtered beasts slides and shudders off

the back of the truck like a job-lot of soiled rugs,
skeins of old rope, old ruptured bagpipes –

they register the triumph of order over passion,
safety over danger, strength over fragility,

and almost seem to climb each other
as though there were somewhere to get: one beast's hoof

stuck in the mouth and the eye-socket
of the one behind it, the rest twisted over, thrown back.

How long, how long it takes a once-living thing
to burn, first it cooks, then is overdone –

two thousand in one trench, in rainy light
through which black smoke hastens up and spreads out

like a dusk of starlings at midday, unignorable drama,
cloudcover tottering on its stem. Think how

it shocks the orderly morning traffic
with too much evidence of process – its fat-crackle.

II

I am the man who wishes to go home now,
who frets, who wakes in night-sweats and whose therapist has

dowsed the ghost-clinging of quadrupeds.
Forgive me, forgive me, whoever is listening

and loves the cloven-hooved. Buried,
I wish my old lugubrious Damascus was buried

in the ground, rusting to a rifle-bore of lacy frills:
raddled wool and sweet breast-meat stopped

its bullets in their flight, stopped and smothered them, left
house after house broken. Forgive me,

all who love the tic-infested. The square-pupilled,
the easily-startled will always look straight into me

even after death. Do sheep – do cattle –
have souls? If so, I fear all I have made is fire

nothing will ever put out, enough centigrade at the core to melt
my belt-buckle and rings while the best of me

is forever burned away in the rivers of
heat, turning the butane-spooks yellow.

III

The pyre is the centre of the whole heath
and burns for days. The men who feed it stare, as if

at a terrible holocaust, or the end of the world;
the heat drives them back and the mud sucks at them

as if even the agents of death are cloven-footed.
Contained by barbed wire, the six hundredth species,

nothing can shift this mountain but fire.
It burns, for days, beneath the skin of the dispossessed,

the tenderer skin of the heath's prison boys...
The bits from it descend like nuclear ash

and settle on every prison-ledge, the exercise yard,
on shoes. They keep the guest houses empty. They speckle

the brilliance of drying sheets. They drift. They float
like giant fish-food on the surface of air.

Perhaps this is the next form a burning carcass
takes, each flake like something coming alive –

a may-fly, a brief thing gulping at light –
jigging awhile over the level lake.

WHY DUNWOODY SMASHED EVERY PANE OF THE STAINED GLASS WINDOW

Dunwoody doesn't know,
so how could I, or anyone?

Maybe because it was dark, from outside,
and its chained indoor rainbow

shut in from him by a giant lock
and that there's something in Dunwoody

which doesn't love a lock – perhaps –
something in him, or me, or we?

Is it him, or me, would like to think
of the churchwarden's silts of anger

stirred into clouds?
Or who'd find the saints false, on breaking in,

and though ending up with dark bottle-bits
prefer the thought, the both of us,

of bright smithereens, a hail of razors
and stalactites, a shattering of stars?

DISTILLING

The stained pillowcases smelling of yeast the clue,
found in the bin, or hurled out from the cell;
...behind the wire human ingenuity
divides like the atom, again and again:
all that pilfered bread kneaded to a mulch through the linen
until there is only the yeast, left
to ferment in a bottle, hidden away for weeks
and flavoured with a little stolen lemon juice
until it begins to bubble, froth and overflow
like Jekyll's test-tubes. *Anything, anything,*
say the distillers, to alter the look of this place,
even this heady, bitter, *undrinkable* brew:
that transforms the average lavatory pan
into Jennifer Aniston's hips, that makes of the pinging out
of six hundred light-bulbs at the same moment
an inhabited darkness, and elongates
the steep perspectives of the cell
into a corridor with somewhere to go.
A brew so potent, the pressure forces off
the stopper, like something coming alive.

PLAYING HANGMAN

Sometimes a word will start it, like
Hands and feet, sun and gloves. The way

Is fraught with danger...
— John Ashbery, *Variant*

The place's favourite game, whose implications reach way down
beneath the founding stones
like roots. They wrap themselves around the chrome

taps, around the porridge bowls, the piss-pots and the mugs.
They have found a way
to the bottom. They are implications. And now must begin to turn up

inside the down-pipe, grabbing hold of sills, of bed-springs,
until they have actually cricked
their necks in every cell, making room by expanding into it.

Every day, at a certain time, when yawns are stifled
and the clatter of locks answers
its own echo, when shoes squeak along the corridors, baffled

to their own array of indistinct reflections that weep away
or deepen according to the mood
of punished boys forced into learning, he gets his chance again:

poor man. Think of him. The half formed man perpetually
trying to come into existence.
Every time his mouth, his hands are drawn, they are as quickly

rubbed out again. He tries again, and again, spared the gallows
before he's a neck to squeeze,
a mouth with which to speak, a toe to sample the shallows.

See how he appears and vanishes, appears and vanishes,
erased into a large red smudge
or scribble of blue, a cloudburst, a smear, a space no longer his:

he's the mouthless puppet to every inmate, whose life depends
upon the counting
of distant Arctic syllables, a counting to the very end

of the guesswork, near misses and ventriloquy
which comprise a broken language.
His life is in the hands, poor man, of that falsetto energy

getting him to act for it, half wishing him to be born,
half wanting him to hang.
It's the donkey-voiced who make him, who scrawl in the outline

that brings him closer to being, now fat, now perilously thin,
now cut off at the waist – a half,
a quarter, a third, an eighth, a tenth of a fully born man

strung up somewhere between his onset and conclusion,
and if that's a half smile
attempting to cross his face it is one for sure flickering in confusion

as he grows from the head down, continuing undeterred
to swing his yet-to-be-formed feet
and discover his name at last – the original, elusive, the *misspelt* word.

LINES FOR THE BIRD THAT FLEW INTO THE PRISON

Against window glass blinded by dust
it dashed itself repeatedly, hovering where it hung
over its own image, beak to beak;
or clung to the blind, in terror, flapping eerily among

our exhausted papers. Strange how it attempted
to fathom the glass, how it drummed a tiny wind an inch
from its liberty – drawn in by our Canaan
of thickening milk and xerox ink.

We guided it with an unmailed letter with which it shared
a destination not-yet-reached
towards the opening, felt its panic,
watched it suddenly hum free, and hold us there –

like it – both curious and perverse;
where tremendous water sucked in reverse.

THE MISSIONARY POSITION

I

Help me, she says, *help me* to unwrap
the violins. Ms Queeper's heart

is a plump, creviced plum. They're brand new,
she says, just delivered to the prison music room.

The men without laces in their shoes
stoop towards her diminutive figure, crouched

over the instruments which are mummified
in bubble-wrap, and start to rip open,

start to pop the bubbles, eager to rip:
pop! pop! pop! they go, in an extempore scale...

each blister a note, a jumping-jack
muted by distance, a tiny release of pressure.

They rip and pull away, rip and pull away
only to find bubble-wrap, more bubble-wrap

and, on the brink, more bubble-wrap;
and where they might expect to find

the violins unscratched and beautiful
there at the tightly wound core: just outable gas, air,

a puff of vapour. Space moulded to the shape
of a conker-smooth, virginal absence.

II

Too slope-shouldered, it was said, too pale,
to go among the burly, indolent sinners –

those eyes ogling her flimsy blouse, the heart beneath
monopolised by God. Too pale,

they said, her fingers too freckle-tactile,
too seeming-not-to-touch-what-they-touched,

the tips of them conducting too tender a static
to go among the easily-electrified.

Too slight, they said, to risk the canopy of grudges
swaying over her, such a chill place to be

at such an hour of the morning.
As it was, well, at the recital, the gap-tooth

and hyperactive, artists of the prison yawn,
sat hugely demure with arms folded tight like men

uncertain of the emotion pedalled to them
while the bow went wading between her knees, as if

sawing her in half. And you might say
they were the selves of which they had a tight grip

while she swayed to a finish, and claps broke out
like a few drops of rain in a tin.

PSYCHOSIS

Because he is older, stronger,
and the other boy smaller and more docile,

he can take into his hands his whole body
(...the body of the mind, that is,

taken in the large hands of the larger mind)
and do to it whatsoever he wishes

as if merely massaging himself, flexing
that awkward ache so troublesome

of late, the cramps he gets in the spaces
in both wrists there between the vital bits, which

he works out through his fingers, answering
the mind's need for the exercise-yard:

all that's left is the smaller one's
flightless body, and him, sated with protein.

THE PHYSICS OF
CHINESE-WRESTLING

When the gulf widens between them
these two young men reach out across it, hand to hand:
the skin of the pulse protests,

the pulse draws back its little egg-head to protest
as if it wants none of this slap
of male upon male. The force of the collision puts

such a strain on each wrist it turns into something else:
a question mark in convulsion,
say, unravelling backwards, a sparrow's stopwatch

ticking in its ribs, an apprentice reaching back over his head
rather than shift the platform –
it is a cradle of ligaments, hoist, the scaffolding that

secures the longing to build, stage by stage.
They bid to the master
builders, and all I know is when another back-of-a-hand

strains towards the table-top or ceiling these two young men
are forming between them
a flying buttress, stone for stone, each one of which

presses against the next to hold the whole building up.
Or else they are forcing
skyward, stone by stone, the walls around them to justify

so wide a roof. Or else, now they are so nearly horizontal,
the building in an act
of upward and equal downward pressure,

of verticals meeting on a level plane, as if impartial,
holds its upright perspective, *just.*
Before falling down all over again.

THE USES OF PEPPER

*"... a carminative, a digestive stimulant, a
passive maker of trade-routes; a balancer of
civilization to rival the Scales of Justice
when placed alongside its uxorious silver
tulip-lip of salt ... a means of keeping the pot-
plants from the moggy piss."*

– William Schwartzman, *The Spice Trade*

And in the joy-riding hands of this young man
an effervescent caster of some spells.
A fine ash from the pepperpot he empties in
the car's interior, while the engine ticks cool – the squalls

that'll scramble the scent in the half mile radius
of police dogs, itch in their million nose-cells;
that'll have them, when the wreck's recovered, recoil
sneezing on their leashes – balking in the rays

which float with it. *Pepper.* Yes, but the sort that gets
to pre-empt discovery, to rub out the traces, to fly:
the cloud of it that ascends to a higher form
of salvation, and hovers there like this:

a freak cumulus snowing softly over
a sunlit, uninhabited, never-visited place.

MUSIC

Cast your palm close
over the bodywork, its swarm of gleams;

speak their names softly, with a sort of reverence:
Prelude, Impreza, Laguna, Celicia....

See how light glances off
their bossy flanks, skidding along the wind-lines;
how their valves close, open to utter
a moderated growl.

But *stolen*, that is the word;
possession, that means, for an hour
which is all they could wish for, like everything in nature
that blooms for a moment,
and withers down, and is incinerated.

        These, says the prison shrink,
are the bumper-wide grins and pedals on which they play
their gaspy symphonies of disaffection.

Afterwards, of course, they must be burned
to so much kettle-black shell
like any thrashed Wurlitzer
never to be played again – any more of it
merely second hand:

        burned in case there remains
the finest split-end of a human hair
or gust of energy or a word
strung from pedal to pedal, or hovering
over the valve like a growl.

GANJA

Watching as Able's big knuckled fingers ply
the strands of his neighbour's hair into tight corn-rows,
stood with the rest, I try bringing to mind what

they most remind me of: the legs of a foal kinking
awkwardly at the knee, the mouths of ten fish
feeding from one source, a cooperation

of cylinders... Now he's returned from the toilet
so suspiciously heavy limbed, the silence around him seems
to have grown a visible aura. Rather than take

the whole class with him where he wants it to go
he follows his finger-bones down, soul and body, down
through ever deepening layers of concentration

to where the receiver – who likes his hair touched – is hung out
like a cuffed kitten which gives up its nape
to such rough licking as this, while way below the eye-line

Able's own two waistbands, turned earthward, loll
like flags from the pole of his spine, one chequered red,
one slipping, standard issue, prison-green.

HYPERACTIVE

A thought flings many limbs,
each of which goes off and comes back laden
with thoughts spilt at twice the rate of yours:

you slowcoaches, you mown and scented men,
he outruns you, yet again. Lock him up, and he
makes of his seven-by-seven cell

a gymnasium of rolling roads, a jogging machine
heading out in every direction:
by the time his many feet run

the first hundred miles, wearing each other out,
by the time his many hands grab hold
of the fire-escape in Blackfriars, vane in Durham,

mast in Gorbals or Ludlow's stopped clock,
(...as light overtakes the cloud-shadow crossing
lumpy vistas of rapeseed) you men

are still tying on your boots,
still aiming the lace at the eye-hole.
Each thought of his is a hare, miles ahead,

which leaves behind the thought-pile
of sky-cycling tortoises with names
and addresses painted on their shells:

from the open country of the mind he sends back
this mad March rejoinder
of teeth, ground-thumps and startled looks,

one eye wide open, one sleepy.

ANATOMY OF THE FLAT

After Nabokov

I

Crowning the subtle camber like the dogmas
of social control, the white line
distinguishing the right from the left side of the road
awaits the wandering ball-joints
or the ghost of Humbert Humbert.
It blurs, wobbles out of shape
in the heat rising from the tarmac, turning
assumption into a torturous rapture,
a harmless plaything, a devil's head
hovering over the broken dashes.
When I drove north (...it is an offence,
says the Traffic Act, section one-o-eight, to cross
the double white line, where the line
nearest you is solid) wind blew
at the microphones, the field birds
swept up in one organic swathe.
Driving north, keeping within the limit,
I could have had no notion of what
giant grill crowned with its V-for-verb
closed like a violent press at speed
upon the wax of my dwarfed insignia,
shortening the miles between us by the second...
the juggernaut and its chassis,
twelve-foot-wide windscreen, its Turin fax
and telephone number printed on the cabin,
bright yellow on green, gold on green.

II

Swaying its assignment of what
might have been oysters steaming in deep freeze
or some unnamed, entirely foreign delicacy
or something semi-transparent, or plasma, sort
of wobbling softly from side to side,
it turned the corner into my path
blasting its fog-horn like a siren
to the amplified gasps of its air-breaks,
the Italian driver cleaving – high up –
to the side of the road presumption and instinct
considered to be his. There was gesticulation,
an instantaneous swapping of mimed oaths through glass.
Both of us turned colours, in an upsurge
of fierce angelic incandescence and surprise
assuming the other had wandered over
and wandered back again then back again
as if to satisfy some special itch.
Braced against the imminence
of terrible collision, the flying off
in all directions of bits – the air-bags
bullying our midriffs into foetuses –
we closed our eyes, and passed through each other
and came out the other side to where
the road was clear, both dreaming
we were headed for the true north
of our own green country.

WATER-WALKING

The judge believes himself to be priestlike,
which is why he's able to talk of wickedness
and at that point, perhaps, judge and priest most rub

up against each other lewdly and seem to be joined
at the ankles. The bits nearest are in focus and the line cuts
through the judge, he and the many like him, who

long since drove the herd of these six hundred men
inside the prison fence. That's why he's able to talk
of wrongdoing, because he feels like he talks on behalf

of the crowds crossing the city square in rain
and the shoe-soles which, every time they come down, find
those of the six hundred rising to meet them

across a vast swimming surface... that's why the saints stooping
either side of him are in focus, so still,
and there are gold thrones in the upper house,

wafers in his hands for the worthless, a kitschery
of lambs and a job lot of old haloes shining back
over his left shoulder, to the vanishing point.

THE FLUTTERING-PLACE

*"Then came the dreams like the popping up of
eerie Spam in the mind's computing, footage
from the subconscious..."*

– Prison Log, *Notes for the Law-abiding*, March 2001

I

Once again the old projector of meaning
is under the dust-sheets, has had to be unplugged

to be saved from the dangers of overload:
the frisks, the classfuls of begrudging prisoners

and a diet of scowls are more than enough
but like any whirring motor it cannot so easily be

switched off or rested and runs on, and my dreams
should not be watched alone in the dark.

Throughout your long and sleeping body, it says, the spools
spin the loaded footage, and have you

lift a knee and an elbow slowly though
you do not know you do, and place your hands

across your sternum tenderly, and blow
your mouth open, twitch your toes. The belly

of dreaming, it says, is the fluttering-place
for frightened birds. With a startled bounce

they flutter back, land, they send up the shiver
that fills the whole projection room.

II

In the midst of the shorn and watchful,
clean collars, which keep in place clean precepts,

clean shirts, which rasp with cleanliness –
as if the prison guards were a speckled mirror –

my hair grows every second, every nanosecond, and has
within minutes spilt across my shoulders

like so much black milk, and my drab clothes changed
into breechclout and scalp-shirt, my pockets stuffed

with huge culpability, potions and pigment-dyes,
feathers of extinct birds, grease paint...

Why should this repeated mandatory *Sir*
oppress more than flatter, have me stood

with downturned mouth and hands to my loins
like Cochise – not, you understand,

out of any sense of inscrutability or pride,
more one of humble surrender –

head down before his captors?
There in the cellar, deep beneath my ankles...

III

...this was not water turned
to wine nor hail to frogs

nor stones to locusts nor any ordinary miracle.
It was the gradual increase of ladybirds

invading every square metre,
filling every square foot, every square inch.

They filled the wide shovels
like brilliant pellets quicker than they could

be shovelled again, as if we used the wrong tools.
There in the cellar, deep beneath my ankles...

They flowed in across the vestibule and down
the step and up the stairs and over the ceilings until

they were the incoming tide and we were merely
shovelling back water, shovelling back water.

I felt, I swear it, like the first tremors,
the whole prison groan up and become an ancient prow,

the foam-edge   of ladybirds
crest like a wave.

IV

...where webs erected a scaffolding
against the retrospective of the cellar's damp

under the weight of prison founding-stones
the fresco was discovered, read in brilliant torch-light

a segment at a time – gold, scarlet, cobalt blue.
Those might have been the feet of athletes

standing in wet grass, with garlands dropped
to the ground, arranged in a perfect composition until

the equator at which the bricks – oozing tongues
of mortar where frost bled a spiky ruff –

took over, slicing them in half at the waist...
a sense, perhaps, of nerve-endings

reaching through the inertia of the wall
to the cortex, aorta, cerebellum

of a phantom upper half... Later, men
were sent down to paint out the fragment

with black emulsion, folding it
in gorgeous nightfall.

V

Like the many with startled eyes, steamed into plastic
and flashed from three dimensions to one

I must, I'm told, endure the prison camera:
my hair by now to my waist, and my choker of crow-beads

elicit a certain curt suspicion while
the Dobermans squeak at my fingers and the guards enact

the strip-search without hands, though I am here to teach.
At length, as all must, I confront the firebox

that takes away our power, I receive the charge
of electrodes, exploded onto the dark...

Running-Man-Flinching-At-The-Indoor-Sun.
Burned into the celluloid, as if burned forever

into my skin, it is the image of a man afraid
of something that hangs in the air, sensing

the faintest suggestion out of what
tobacco-pouches are made in these parts.

There beneath my ankles, deep beneath my bootsoles
a stifled, shamanistic yelp.

AT DUSK, YOU CAN HEAR
THE MEN CALLING

The voices calling from cell windows
are like those held in the answerphone,
they fill the house, hopeful someone might speak back
but meet instead the infinite scope

for confession, hope, evasion and doubt,
self-entanglement, scorn – a crack
in the reinforced wall of silence.
At dusk the voices are almost eerie,

like the sound of drowning men far out at sea.
They fill the whole empty house
of the air and the trees and the heathland, aimed
with light's last dregs and onset of cold

at someone who is or is not listening either
on the next block or in the next world.

GROUND BASS

*"Having confessed to the killing of some fifty five people,
though adjudged legally sane, created – it has been said – by
the excesses of Soviet famine and deprivation, Chikatilo was
taken to the Serbsky Institute in Moscow for psychiatric
evaluation..."* – New York Times, October 1992

Don't talk to me of the soul; that after all
is the business of saints. Do you imagine it squats
on the shelf, thick with the beautiful references?

I think it moves the left half of the brain which moves
the right, etcetera. Through your two-way glass,
gentlemen, I was the wrong way around,

and though the left half of the brain is held responsible
for the actions of the right half of the body
I was confused as to what was left,

what right, what normally sloped one way
sloping the other. That mouth. Oh, I note your eyes
slip away in one movement and look down

as you throw a leg across the other, and sigh,
and brush your sleeves... windblown
and still recovering from the eleven flights

which lead you down, not up, and place
such a strain upon the muscles of the calf...
better, though, perhaps than that

secateurs of a lift (I see you smile)
which brings you down, down through the centre
of this old building by the light

of a flickering forty watt bulb which still
somehow refuses to blow.
                              I cause, I know,
       your keyboards to click more avidly of late,

tracking white with bright ideas or shunting
the carriages which jostle and bump
and stall behind the cursor's engine

towards the slow ascent and descent
of understanding. I am the stump in mist
even your rainswell cannot dislodge

when everything floods like the yellow Grushevska
roaring at such a speed it swept away
and then washed up the evidence;

what I had sent out was brought back,
brought back, and ducked me towards
the final enfilade of flash-cubes in the snow:

Chikatilo the frozen. Prize of the Public
Prosecutor's Office. They say I have two souls.
One plausible tenth, they say, Andrei Romanovich

shows us by the light of day
while the other nine are out of sight...
You must forgive me. Your appetite of course

is one that has no bottom at all,
as if with each fresh morsel, full of protein,
the stone in the belly is appeased

but never fully satisfied, being stonelike.
Little Lena Zakotnova, Larisa Tkachenko,
bewildered Lyuba Biryuk in her thirteenth year,

Ivan Beletski picking apricots in sunlight
and the other fifty-one who strolled too close
to the centre, who rolled over one by one

in their skeins of drenched hair,
cling to my belt-buckle, cuffs, my fingertips.
The mortician's label is attached to their toes.

Should I continue? I think there is
something of the prurient priest at large
in your questioning, offended by what

most attracts and is enough to drop
your young assistant's elbow on the zero-key
of the machine which trundled in his lap

but now sends out (though he doesn't know it)
a flat line of zeros across the screen
beyond the last recorded intelligence

while he sips at his mug with startled eyes:
how is he to know, when the succession of noughts
suddenly jumps onto its second line

and then a third and then a fourth and fifth,
language has failed, and a new sort of wilderness
is being created as it is discovered

a centimetre at a time, offering no
distinguishing features or signs of life,
just more, just more and more of the same?

I give you what you most seem to want;
I give you what I give you.
                              The lift goes down.
I grew, that is to say, I grew there

in growth-spurts of infinite slowness
far from the dangerous surface:
beneath the upper light my glacial will

was legumes of stretched rock, so long
and tapering, like organ pipes sipping frozen water,
and the mile of my small intestine

wound down, down, in rock-folds
smooth as marble or polished obsidian
towards the crystal cave of the duodenum

thick with a white profusion
of snow-flowers along to the holly-like nibs of which
a gathering plump drip rolled

its undiluted acid – and froze:
the unusually developed (...it is said)
cerebellum bloomed in an overhead drapery

of frozen folia, shedding a fine frost...
Your lamps shine into me. I am
the spectacular efflorescence

of your spirit's boredom. Note how
your voices drop in my company
like Sunday hats removed in reverence, how

the fishmonger treasures my till receipt
and others my clippings, a single hair, a relic,
any faintest, obscurest relic of me

while the crowds trail past my door
as if my rarity were the wonder
and a certain sort of status conferred

by touching it, even by drawing close.
You greet me, shall we say, somewhere between
curiosity and fear – disturbed and intrigued

by a man with knowledge of the depths.
I grew too slowly,
                    while everything sped.
When the world developed requirements

it could neither articulate nor meet
I knew I had grown out of want
and I knew I had grown slowly enough

to do the dirty work, to wring the surplus
of moisture from Christ's sponge
though your hands, shall we say, were clean... it must

be fine to sit in your self-angelising
seat, clean-cuffed and manicured, confident your hands
will never be grubbied, shuffling papers...

When I lift my left foot in its chains
a tram stalls in rainy Rostov, then starts again.
Shortly, gentlemen, you'll squeal your chair-legs

and depart, gathering up your effects
and rewinding your machine, leaving me
to the very last of my several attempts

to prolong the conversation... words dissolving
with my latest expression, fade by fade,
though held in your magnetic signal

like the voice from the other side, to be
played over and over for the clue.
Tape me a moment longer, though your eyes betray

involvement inflected with unease,
a weariness laced with tact....
What of the age, I ask you, which demands a beast

more slyly itself, more extravagant,
to manage needs so complex?
I felt my acts drawn larger, as if a pantograph

first set down the point that followed
every crevice and outline of each act
while the second point, as if instructed,

enlarged it perhaps some twenty times:
and the arms that linked the two pistoned back
and plunged like mechanical elbows

on their swivelling rivets; so both continued
moving as one, faithful to every detail
the first discovered at the tip of its point

and the second merely reproduced,
until the gadget completed the outline both
of the act and its intricate implications

the more you looked, as if you looked through
the atoms at exploded atoms beneath
and saw some terrible truth there.

Sometimes I dreamt it was God.
Or perhaps a minor, unassuming god
sometimes inclined to whisper a little

of the flame that could burn a halo
out of these zero temperatures
– now orange, now yellow, now blue –

or flare up, of a sudden, like caught gas
and burn away my stained cape,
and burn away my hands, and burn away my feet,

and burn away my body out of which
a body might grow, warmed on one side
to a sort of rosy flush by the flame

that infuses crystal with creeping colour
and bursts from the frozen heart itself
and fills my mouth.

Acknowledgements

Acknowledgements are due to the editors of the following maga-
zines and newspapers in which some of these poems first
appeared or will appear: *Ambit, Ars Interpres (Stockholm), Arts
Council England Writers' Awards Anthology 2003, Hard Times (Berlin),
The Independent, Leviathan Quarterly, New Welsh Review, The North,
Poetry Book Society Bulletin, PN Review, Poetry London, Poetry Review,
Poetry Wales, Priora, Stand Magazine, Thumbscrew.*

Twelve of the poems in this book were first published as a short
pamphlet entitled *The Uses of Pepper,* one of the winners of The
Poetry Business Book and Pamphlet Competition 2002-2003. As
a collection-in-progress this book (or rather fourteen of the
poems contained in it) won an Arts Council England Writers'
Award in April 2003. 'For the Seven Hundred and Forty Ninth
Species of Barbed Wire', 'The Language School', 'The Uses of
Pepper' and 'The Blood Choir' appeared in the anthology which
resulted from that award. The last named of these poems first
appeared under a different title and has subsequently been much
revisited. 'For the Seven Hundred and Forty Ninth Species of
Barbed Wire' also appeared in the Poetry Calendar 2006, edited
by Shafiq Naz and produced by Alhambra Publishing, Belgium,
and will appear in *Priora*, curated and photographed by Kitty
Sullivan and edited by James Byrne, (Phaidon, 2007).

I am very grateful for the Hawthornden Fellowship (April-May,
2002) during the expansive space of which new poems were writ-
ten, older poems revisited and this book first brought together.
Without this time, the manuscript begun at Hawthornden would
have taken a good deal longer to complete. I would also like to
extend my gratitude to my employers at Bath Spa University for
the teaching relief in 2005 which enabled me to complete the
mannuscript; and to my employers at the Young Offenders' Prison
in question: firstly for employing me; secondly for supporting me
throughout a long year. I'd also like to thank the large number of
inmates I taught during that year, without whom this book would
have very little to talk about. I dedicate it to them.

The book was extremely fortunate to benefit from the advice of several readers. Special thanks are due to Gerard Woodward and Richard Kerridge for their meticulous close reading and innumerable suggestions; to Fiona Sampson, particularly, for the rigour of her repeated readings from the onset of the project; and to Peter Porter for his wisdom, his counsel and very particular encouragement. And finally to Miranda Liardet for her energy and ebullient support. The book is for her.